REPORT TO TH

C000016552

087459

Savings Available If Shipping Containers For Military Electronic Equipment Are Reused

8-146917

Department of the Army

BY THE COMPTROLLER *GENERAL* OF THE UNITED STATES

770282/
087459

FEB.15,1968

B-146917

To the President of the Senate and the
Speaker of the House of Representatives

The General Accounting Office has reviewed the utilization by the Department of the Army of reusable containers for electronic equipment. This report presents our findings and the corrective actions taken by the Army on our proposals.

We found a need for improvement in the Army's procedures for identifying containers and making them available for transfer to manufacturers of electronic equipment for the shipment of newly produced electronic equipment. Such use of Government-furnished shipping containers would aid materially in reducing procurement costs,

From June 1962 through July 1965, the Army purchased various types of shipping and storage containers even though similar reusable containers valued at about $1.1 million were available in Army depots at the time the procurements were made. During the same period, reusable containers valued at about $327,000 were disposed of. We found that containers were not being utilized because Army procedures did not require procurement and supply personnel to coordinate their efforts and identify containers already available in the Army supply system.

We discussed the potential utilization of containers with appropriate Army officials during our review and pointed out specific instances in which these containers could be supplied to contractors as Government-furnished material. In response, the Army did furnish containers valued at $489,880 to various contractors.

In commenting on our findings and proposals, the Deputy Assistant Secretary of Defense (Supply and Services) agreed in October 1967 that additional actions must be taken to improve the management of reusable containers for all types of equipment. He informed us that controls over the management of such containers at the various Army Commands would be assessed and revised as necessary. He also stated that all the military services and the Defense Supply Agency had been directed to conduct a review and to correct any deficiencies found. In future audit, work, we will inquire into the effectiveness and adequacy of the corrective actions taken,

National Defense: Savings Available If Shipping Containers for Military Electronic Equipment Are Reused: B-146917

U.S. Government Accountability Office (GAO)

The BiblioGov Project is an effort to expand awareness of the public documents and records of the U.S. Government via print publications. In broadening the public understanding of government and its work, an enlightened democracy can grow and prosper. Ranging from historic Congressional Bills to the most recent Budget of the United States Government, the BiblioGov Project spans a wealth of government information. These works are now made available through an environmentally friendly, print-on-demand basis, using only what is necessary to meet the required demands of an interested public. We invite you to learn of the records of the U.S. Government, heightening the knowledge and debate that can lead from such publications.

Included are the following Collections:

Budget of The United States Government
Presidential Documents
United States Code
Education Reports from ERIC
GAO Reports
History of Bills
House Rules and Manual
Public and Private Laws

Code of Federal Regulations
Congressional Documents
Economic Indicators
Federal Register
Government Manuals
House Journal
Privacy act Issuances
Statutes at Large

We are reporting these matters to the Congress because of the potential for significant improvement in the management and use of reusable containers.

Copies of this report are being sent to the Director, Bureau of the Budget: the Secretary of Defense; and the Secretary of the Army.

Comptroller General
of the United States

Contents

REPORT ON

SAVINGS AVAILABLE IF SHIPPING

CONTAINERS FOR MILITARY

ELECTRONIC EQUIPMENT ARE REUSED

DEPARTMENT OF THE ARMY

INTRODUCTION

The General Accounting Office has examined into the utilization by the Department of the Army of certain types of reusable containers (transit cases) for electronic equipment. Our examination, made pursuant to the Budget and Accounting Act, 1921 (31 U.S.C. 53), and the Accounting and Auditing Act of 1950 (31 U.S.C. 67), was directed primarily toward those matters apparently needing attention in the management of containers, and it did not include an overall evaluation of the management of inventories by the Army Electronics Command.

We examined records and reports on the utilization of reusable containers for selected electronic equipment procured during the period June 1962 through July 1965. We completed our review in November 1967. Our examination was made at the United States Army Electronics Command, Fort Monmouth, New Jersey, and Philadelphia, Pennsylvania; the Tobyhanna Army Depot, Tobyhanna, Pennsylvania; the Lexington-Blue Grass Army Depot, Lexington, Kentucky; and the Sacramento Army Depot, Sacramento, California.

The reuse of containers has been a continuing problem in the Department of Defense. We previously reported on similar situations in the Navy in July 1964 and February 1965 (B-146917).

BACKGROUND

A transit case is a reusable container which is procured in varying sizes and weights. It consists of an outer shell and a cover. A liner, which is usually suspended by springs within the case is required to protect the contents from shock during shipment. (See photograph on p. 2.) Hereinafter, transit cases are referred to as containers. Initially, these containers were intended to house electronic components during shipment, storage, and usage.

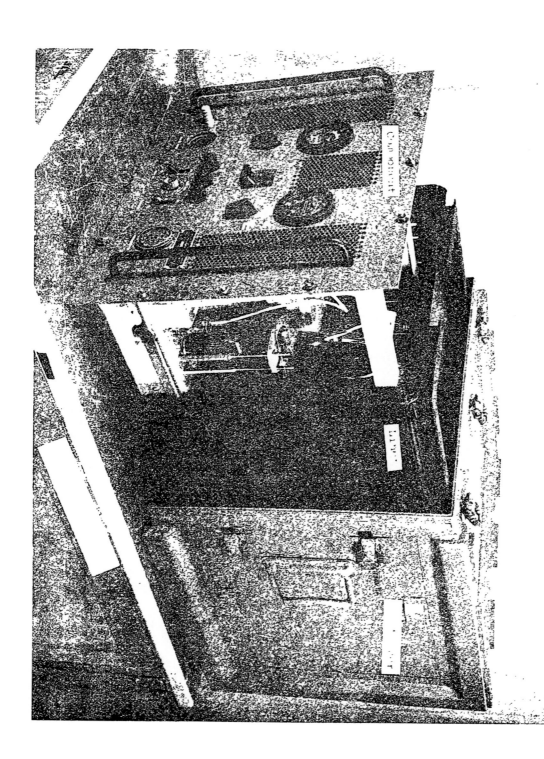

POWER SUPPLY PP-685 A/TRC
PART OF AN/TRC-24

In September 1960 a procedure was instituted which provided for the removal of the components from containers for installation into shelters and for the reutilization of cases as Government-furnished shipping containers. A shelter is generally constructed of metal, is large enough to house the completely assembled electronic equipment: and operating personnel, and is usually transported by helicopter or truck, Because of the shelter program, containers are now being used primarily as shipment containers.

The United States Army Electronics Command (ECOM)--a major subcommand of the United States Army Materiel Command (AMC)--is responsible for the research, design, development, testing, and supply management of electronic equipment, including those components which are shipped and stored in containers.

The Procurement and Production Directorate of ECOM is responsible for procuring electronic equipment and for providing necessary engineering support. The Materiel Readiness Directorate is responsible for management of worldwide inventory and maintenance of electronic equipment for the Army.

The containers included in our review are used for components of the AN/TRC-24, AN/TTC-7A, AN/TCC-3, AN/TTC-7, TA-182/u, and TH-5/TG electronic systems.

A list of the principal officials of the Department of Defense and the Department of the Army responsible for the administration of activities discussed in this report is shown in appendix I.

IMPROVEMENT NEEDED EN PROCEDURES FOR UTILIZING REUSABLE CONTAINERS

Improvement was needed in the Army's procedures for identifying available containers for electronic equipment so that the containers could be utilized as Government-furnished material in connection with future procurements.

Prom June 1962 through July 1965, the Army procured containers costing about $2.2 million even though similar containers valued at about $1.1 million were on hand in Army depots and could have been furnished to contractors at the time the procurements were made. Furthermore, during the same period, containers valued at about $327,001) were disposed of which could have been utilized. Our review indicated that the containers were not furnished to the contractors because ECOM's procedures did not require procurement and supply personnel to coordinate their efforts and identify containers that were in the supply system.

On September 30, 1960, the Department of the Amy notified ECOM that, because of increased emphasis on mobility in the field, most communication electronic equipment would thereafter be mounted in shelters, making it unnecessary to use the shipping containers in the field. In May 1962 the Army directed all field organizations to return to the storage depots containers that would become available as a result of the shelter installation program, stating that they were urgently needed to be furnished to contractors as shipping containers.

We discussed the utilization of containers with ECOM personnel in August 1964 and later identified specific instances in which available containers could be furnished to contractors. Subsequently, the Army did furnish containers valued at $489,000 to various contractors, but we noted additional instances in which cases were still being procured even though similar items were available. A summary of the values of containers available during the period June 30, 1962, through July 30, 1965, is shown as appendix 11.

Further details of our findings follow.

Reusable containers not utilized effectively

During our review,, we identified about 54,000 units of different types of containers stored at the Tobyhanna, Lexington, and Sacramento Army depots, many of which could

4

have been utilized in lieu of new procurements. These containers, valued at over $2 million were used primarily for shipping components of AN/TRC-24, AN/TTC-7A, AN/TCC-3, AN/TTC-7, TA-182/u, and TH-5/TG electronic equipment, Some examples follow.

1. Seven contracts had been awarded by ECQM from August 1962 through March 1964 for the procurement of components of the AN/TRC-24, including containers valued at about $993,000. Even though similar cases valued at about $600,000 were available at the time procurements were initiated, they were not furnished to any of the contractors, For example, 1,476 cases (Federal stock number 5820-392-8077) were procured with the AN/TRC-24 radio set in August 1962. At the time of the procurement, 1,221 of these containers were available in depot stock and could have been supplied to the contractor, In July and August 1964, a large quantity of containers for components of the AN/TRC-24 were available, and in some instances the containers were being donated to several States or were being disposed of at a fraction of their initial cost. This set utilizes 13 different types of containers, (See app. III.)

2. In January 1965 containers for AN/TTC-7A components valued at about $91,000 were in stock at Tobyhanna. At that time, ECOM issued a solicitation for bids for additional AN/TTC-7As, including containers valued at about $58,000. We called this fact to the attention of management personnel at Tobyhanna in January 1965 and they advised ECOM that available containers could be utilized. ECOM subsequently advised us that the containers had not been used because they had bean assigned temporary control numbers instead of Federal stock numbers and ECOM had. been unable to identify them as being applicable to the AN/TTC-7A. (See p. 6 for further: discussion.)

Need for improved procedures for
determining availability of containers

ECOM procedures did not require the inventory managers to ascertain whether containers were available prior to the procurement of electronic equipment. Under ECOM procedures, stock availability data are compared with procurement parts lists to determine what items can be furnished to contractors. These parts lists indicate the various components and subassemblies of the items being procured, but we found that containers were not separately shown (except those for components of the AN/TRC-24). In many instances, therefore, ECOM personnel could not identify applicable containers and could not determine whether available stocks of containers could be supplied to contractors. As a result, new containers were being purchased.

Shipping containers for the AN/TRC-24 were listed on the parts lists but the stock on hand was not utilized because the lists were not reviewed by ECOM personnel. They apparently had requested the parts lists from the ECOM library but had not received them. In addition to the parts lists, however, there are other publications which show the components for electronic equipment; but ECOM procedures did not require a review of other available publications.

There was also a need for improved guidance in ECOM's procedures for identification and utilization of containers without liners. Liners are required within the cases to protect the components from shock during shipment. Since the containers without liners were not separately reported from those with liners, the entire stock of containers was considered as not being available for contractor utilization.

In September 1966 there were in stock $1.5 million worth of containers, both with and without liners, for the AN/TRC-24, which could have been utilized. However, ECOM's procedures did not provide for the depots either to separately identify reusable containers with liners so that they could be used or to determine the practicability of fabricating or procuring liners separately for those containers for which no liners were on hand.

Many of the containers were eventually authorized for disposal because they did not have liners. For example, records at Tobyhanna showed that about 3,200 containers for the AN/TRC-24 were disposed of during fiscal years 1963, 1964, and 1965 because they had no liners. Most of these cases could have been furnished to contractors during fiscal years 1965 and 1966 if new liners had been obtained. Generally, those cases disposed of either were donated to various State governments or were sold for a fraction of their cost.

Complete asset identification not obtained

ECOM was not able to identify the availability of some containers because they were stored in depots under depot control numbers rather than Federal stock numbers (FSNs).

Our examination showed that 1,014 reusable containers, valued at $110,000 had been assigned depot control numbers and were therefore not identified a5 being available when new cases were procured. For example, in January 1965 we suggested to ECOM that certain containers be furnished to contractors. ECOM, however, was unable to identify and utilize these cases because they had not been assigned FSNs and descriptive data had not been requested Prom the depots, As a result 700 new containers were procured at a cost of $58,000 although similar containers were in depot stock, Tobyhanna disposed of 193 units of one type for about $318,while 210 of the same type were being procured at a cost of $46,200.

Prior to February 1, 1965, if material was delivered to an Army depot but was not identified by an FSN, the depot would assign its own identification numbers for stock control purposes. Since that date the responsibility for assigning control numbers and for maintaining the descriptive data has been delegated to ECOM. In September 1966 we were informed that ECOM personnel had been assigned to review and identify all major items assigned depot control numbers, including containers, in order to determine what stocks were on hand in the depots.

<u>Evaluation of internal audit</u>

We examined into the work performed by the Army Audit Agency (AAA) in the area of supply management. We found that AAA had issued a special report on its Audit of Supply Management at ECOM on March 15, 1965. This audit had been made for the primary purpose of evaluating the effectiveness with which ECOM accomplished the supply management of repair parts.

One section of this report dealing with the utilization of transit cases, stated:

"A combination of unresolved, long-standing problems concerning major component transit cases and inadequate coordination between the PEMA Division and the Stock Fund Division has: (i) precluded the use of major component outer metal cases and covers as Government-furnished property (GFP); (ii) resulted in significant usable quantities being excessed; (iii) made the proper identification of incomplete cases difficult and expensive because of incorrect condition reservation classification ***."

We were advised that ECOM had taken certain specific actions in response to the conditions reported by the Army Audit Agency. Our review indicated, however, that further improvement in the management of containers was needed. The Army agreed that additional actions were required and stated that controls and procedures at all commodity commands would be revised as necessary.

- - - -

We have in the past reported on other instances where available reusable containers have not been advantageously utilized to fill existing requirements. In one instance, the available containers were disposed of and procurements were made to satisfy existing requirements by the Navy. In another instance, procurement of containers was initiated by the Navy for existing requirements when there were cases already available in the supply system. These matters are contained in our reports of February 1965 and July 1964, respectively (B-146917).

In our prior reports we made recommendations for improvements, and corrective actions were taken or initiated. We believe, however, that the prior cases, coupled with the matters discussed in this report, show the need for management personnel to look into possibilities for increased

utilization of containers at all other inventory control
points in the military services.

Agency comments

There was general agreement on the need to improve the
management of containers **after** we brought these matters to
the attention of the Secretary of Defense on August 7,
1967, and actions were taken or initiated, as discussed be-
low. We were advised, however, that the Army did not agree
with our estimates of the potential **savings which** might
have been realized through better utilization of containers. Specifically, the Department of Defense commented:

> "**Many** of the containers involved were without
> liners **and** it has been found that in such cases
> the **cost** of providing liners and **of** bringing the
> containers **up to** usable conditions **often** closely
> approaches **or exceeds the cost of** procuring new
> containers complete **with liners."**

During the course of our review, ECOM officials stated
that it was uneconomical to either fabricate or procure new
liners for those containers not having liners. **When** we requested cost data in support of this opinion, however, we
were advised that ECOM had no cost estimates for in-house
fabrication of liners. Moreover, we found that in the **past**
the Army had, on at least one occasion, obtained a limited
number of **separate liners in order** to utilize available
containers.

We recognize that the costs of procuring or fabricat-
ing a small number of liners could exceed the costs of new
containers with liners, We believe, however, that the potential savings **inherent** in the acquisition of a large
quantity of liners **to** facilitate the reutilization of
available containers valued at over $1 million could have
been substantial, In our opinion, the possible savings
warranted greater management attention than was given to
this problem,

Recommendations and agency actions

In view of the need for improvement in the management
of reusable containers, we recommend in line with our proposals brought to the attention of the Secretary of Defense
on August 7, 1967, that (I) the **Secretary of the Army** take
appropriate actions to improve the **management** of reusable
containers for electronic equipment and (2) the Office of
the Secretary of Defense consider the need for a Defense-
wide review and evaluation at other appropriate inventory

control points of their procedures regarding the **recovery and reutilization** of shipping **and/or** storage containers.

The Deputy Assistant Secretary of Defense **(Supply** and **Services),** by **letter** dated **October** 16, 1967 **(copy** included as **app. IV)** commented on our findings and proposals. In **general,** he informed us that the Army agreed that additional actions must be taken to **improve** the management of reusable containers, not just at the Army Electronics **Command,** but at all other Army commodity commands. To ensure that improvements are made, controls **and procedures** in effect at these commands will be **assessed and** revised **as** necessary. **The** Deputy Assistant Secretary **also** informed **us** that all the military services and the **Defense** Supply Agency had been directed to conduct **a** review of their procedures for recovery and utilization of containers and to correct any deficiencies uncovered.

We will inquire into the effectiveness **and** adequacy **of these** actions in **our** future audit work.

APPENDIXES

PRINCIPAL OFFICIALS OF THE

DEPARTMENT OF DEFENSE AND THE

DEPARTMENT OF THE ARMY

RESPONSIBLE FOR ADMINISTRATION OF

ACTIVITIES DISCUSSED IN THIS REPORT

	Tenure of office	
	From	To

DEPARTMENT OF DEFENSE

SECRETARY OF DEFENSE:
Robert S. McNamara	Jan. 1961	Present

DEPUTY SECRETARY OF DEFENSE:
Paul H. Nitze	July 1967	Present
Cyrus R. Vance	Jan, 1964	June 1967

ASSISTANT SECRETARY OF DEFENSE (INSTALLATIONS AND LOGISTICS):
Thomas D. Morris	Sept. 1967	Present
Paul R Ignatius	Dec. 1964	Aug. 1967
Thomas D. Morris	Jan, 1961	Dec. 1964

DEPARTMENT OF THE ARMY

SECRETARY OF THE ARMY:
Stanley R. Resor	July 1965	Present
Stephen Ailes	Jan. 1964	July 1965

UNDER SECRETARY OF THE ARMY:
David E. McGiffert	July 1965	Present
Stanley R. Resor	Mar. 1965	July 1965
Vacant	Dec. 1964	Mar. 1965
Paul R. Ignatius	Mar, 1964	Dec. 1964

ASSISTANT SECRETARY OF THE ARMY (INSTALLATIONS AND LOGISTICS):
Dr. Robert A. Brooks	Oct. 1965	Present
Daniel. M. Luevano	July 1964	Oct. 1965

CHIEF OF STAFF, UNITED STATES ARMY:
Gen. Harold K. Johnson	July 1964	Present

PRINCIPAL OFFICIALS OF THE

DEPARTMENT OF DEFENSE AND THE

DEPARTMENT OF THE ARMY

RESPONSIBLE FOR ADMINISTRATION OF

ACTIVITIES DISCUSSED IN THIS REPORT (continued)

	Tenure of office	
	From	To

DEPARTMENT OF THE ARMY (continued)

	From	To
DEPUTY CHIEF OF STAFF *FOR* LOGISTICS:		
Lt. Gen. Lawrence 3. Lincoln, Jr.	Aug. 1964	Present
COMMANDING GENERAL, UNITED STATES ARMY MATERIEL COMMAND:		
Gen. Frank S. Besson, Jr.	July 1962	Present

SUMMARY OF VALUES OF CONTAINERS

FUR THE PERIOD

JUNE 30, 1962, TO JULY 30, 1965

| Electronic equipment | Value of procurements | | Total |
	Prior to August 1964	Subsequent to August 1964	
AN/TRC-24	$ 992,950	$362,790	$1,355,740
Less disposals			
AN/TTC-7A	136,130	58,100	194,230
AN/TCC-3	260,850	-	260,850
AN/TTC-7	84,650		84,650
TA-182/u	247,590	-	247,590
TH-5/TG	30,720	-	30,720
	$1,752,890	$420,890	$2,173,780

[a]Cases furnished subsequent to August 1964; none prior to that date.

| Value of cases available as GFP not furnished | | | Value of cases |
Prior to August 1964	Subsequent to August 1964	Total	furnished as GFP (note a)
$ 600,250	$352,530	$ 952,780	$397,410
	327,210	327,210	
600,250	25,320	625,570	
51,730	58,100	109,830	28,010
93,080	—	93,080	64,000
74,280	—	74,280	—
181,260	—	181,260	—
30,720	—	30,720	—
$1,031,320	$ 83,420	$1,114,740	$489,420

REUSABLE CONTAINERS INCLUDED IN OUR EXAMINATION

Federal stock number		Corresponding management control number (note a)	Electronic equipment
5820–264–7568			AN/TRC-24
5820–284–0357	(note b)	5820–G54–0675	
5820–295–7125			
5820–392–8074		5820–G54–0678	
5820–392–8075	[note b)	5820–G54–0679	
5820–392–8076			
5820–392–8077			
5820–392–8078			
5820–393–2030		5820–G54–0677	
5820–504–7187		5820–G54–0133	
5820–510–4759)	(note b)	5820–G54–0674	
5820–537–7899)		5820–G54–0676	
5820–566–4915			
5805–392–8080			AN/TTC-7A
5805–392–8081			
5805–534–3052			
5805–545–8242			
		5805–G51–0019) (note c)	
		5805–G53–2314)	
		5805–G98–4861) (note c)	
		5805–G53–2312)	
		5805–G98–4862) (note c)	
		5805–G53–2310)	
		5805–G98–4863) (note c)	
		5805–G53–2303)	
		5805–G98–4864) (note c)	
		5805–G53–2311)	
5805–306–2309		5805–G54–1951	
5805–306–2310		5805–G54–1888	AN/TCC-3, AN/TTC-7
5805–306–2311		5805–G54–1938	
6130–284–0358			
5805–682–951.1			TA-182/u, TH-5/TG

[a]G51 and G98 designate Tobyhanna Army Depot.
G53 designates Lexington Army Depot.
G54 designates Sacramento Army Depot.

[b]Included in AAA report No. PH–65–25.

[c]Identical case6 stored in different depots,

ASSISTANT SECRETARY OF DEFENSE
WASHINGTON, D.C. 20301

16 OCT 1967

SR
INSTALLATIONS AND LOGISTICS

Mr. William A. Newman, Jr.
Director, Defense Division
General Accounting Office
Washington, D.C. 20548

Dear Mr. Newman:

Reference is made to your letter of August 7, 1967 which forwarded
for review and comment a draft report on utilization of reusable
shipping containers for electronic equipment by the Department of
the Army (OSD Case #2640).

The report states that additional costs of $1.4 million were incurred
at the Army Electronics Command (ECOM) in the period June 30, 1962
to July 30, 1965 because ECOM, through procedural deficiencies, did
not provide available transit cases as government furnished property
(GFP) to contractors. The report also indicates that these deficiencies
were pointed out in an Army Audit Agency (AAA) report, but that no
corrective action was taken prior to the time of your review. You
recommend to the Secretary of the Army that action be taken by ECOM
to assure more effective management of reusable transit containers
and that the Commanding General, ECOM, re-emphasize the need to take
timely and positive corrective action on findings and recommendations
of internal audits.

The Army agrees that additional actions must be taken to improve the
management of reusable containers, not just at ECOM, but at all
commodity commands. To assure that these improvements are made, controls and procedures in effect at these commands will be assessed and
revised as necessary.

The Army does not agree with your contentions as to the possible
savings which might have been incurred through better utilization of
containers. Many of the containers involved were without liners and
it has been found that in such cases the cost of providing liners and
of bringing the containers up to usable conditions often closely
approaches or exceeds the cost of procuring new containers complete
with liners.

[See GAO note.]

In regard to your final recommendation that the Office of the Secretary of Defense consider the need for a Defense-wide review of this area, all of the Services and DSA have been directed to conduct a review and correct any deficiencies uncovered.

Sincerely,

PAUL H. RILEY
Deputy Assistant Secretary of Defense
(Supply and Services)

GAO Note: **Comments relating to internal audit deleted in that the report recognizes that ECOM has taken certain specific actions on findings of internal audit,**